THE BOSTON TEA PARTY

A HISTORY PERSPECTIVES BOOK

Linda Crotta Brennan

Published in the United States of America by Sleeping Bear Press
Ann Arbor, Michigan
www.sleepingbearpress.com

Consultants: Robert J. Allison, PhD, Chair and Professor, Department
of History, Suffolk University; Marla Conn, ReadAbility, Inc.
Editorial direction: Red Line Editorial

Photo Credits: Library of Congress, cover (left), cover (right), 1 (left), 1 (right), 21;
North Wind Picture Archives/AP Images, cover (middle), 1 (middle); Sarony & Major/
Library of Congress, cover, title; Sleeping Bear Press, 4; North Wind Picture Archives, 7,
10, 13, 14, 17, 22, 24, 28, 30

ISBN 978-1-58536-900-3

Printed in the United States of America
Corporate Graphics Inc.

10 9 8 7 6 5 4 3 2 1

TABLE OF CONTENTS

In this book, you will read about the Boston Tea Party from three perspectives. Each perspective is based on real things that happened to real people who lived in or near Boston in 1773. As you'll see, the same event can look different depending on one's point of view.

Ann Clerk
Colonial Merchant's Wife

England tells us colonists the cost of the French and Indian War was high. The **Seven Years' War**, as they called it in England, dragged on and on against the French, finally ending in 1763.

In the end, England won the war and gained French Canada, Spanish Florida, and parts of India. Now **Parliament** needs us to pay taxes to cover the cost of sending British soldiers here to defend the colonies and frontiers. This makes perfect sense to me. Taxes are paid in England, and our American men pay taxes that are collected by our own elected assemblies. We should also pay for the protection offered by these soldiers. But some colonists feel no need to pay the taxes or duties the British Parliament collects. They have **smuggled** goods, tax free, for a long time without penalty.

I, like many here in the colonies, remain loyal to England and my king. Aren't we of English stock? My great-grandparents were born in England. And the British soldiers did us service. They protected us from the raids of the French and their Indian allies. It is reasonable that we should pay for that protection through taxes to Parliament.

THINK ABOUT IT

▶ Determine the main point of this paragraph and pick out one piece of evidence that supports it.

5

SECOND SOURCE

▶ Find another source on the Stamp Act and compare the information provided there to the information in this source.

Others don't agree with me though. When the British Parliament enacted the **Stamp Act** back in 1765, there was an uproar. The law put a tax on all printed material, from newspapers to playing cards. These items were stamped as proof that the tax was paid. It was the first time we colonists had been taxed directly by England. Before, only our local **legislatures** here in the colonies had directly taxed us. There was great outcry against "taxation without representation." You see, colonists have no representatives in the British Parliament. People found it unfair that Parliament could vote to tax us when colonists did not have a voice in Parliament. I doubt the protesters would have been happy if we had been given representation. It was the tax they hated—money out of their greedy pockets.

▲ *Colonists protested against the Stamp Act.*

Boston's Sons of Liberty were born out of anger against this tax. Even my dear brother, James Hopkins, joined them. He has penned many an essay defending the colonists' rights. He argues that we are the equals of Englishmen living in England. We should be given a say in creating the laws that affect us.

THE SONS OF LIBERTY

The Sons of Liberty was a patriot organization originally formed to fight the Stamp Act. It probably began in Boston and New York. Eventually, it spread through all 13 colonies. The group organized protests against British rule.

The Sons of Liberty called to **boycott** English goods. My husband, Edward, who runs a small shop, saw a large drop in sales. It almost ruined us. The merchants back in England didn't fare well either. They made a complaint to Parliament, and the Stamp Act was repealed.

Then Parliament came up with the Townshend Acts, which included new taxes on glass, lead, and paint. The most hated tax of all was the tax against tea. The beverage is a favorite with rich and poor alike. The Sons of Liberty called for another boycott. The people found a substitute—a drink brewed from an American plant. It doesn't satisfy like real tea though.

These Townshend Acts were also repealed— but the tax on tea remained. Parliament would not give way here. It wanted to prove it had a right to tax all British subjects, whether they lived in England or abroad.

▲ *Colonists found ways to avoid buying British goods, such as spinning their own wool to avoid purchasing British clothes.*

Next Parliament passed the Tea Act. Its purpose was to aid the **East India Company**. Only the East India Company and their chosen merchants could sell tea in our town. We could no longer import tea from the Dutch or French. The East India Company had so much tea, it could be sold at a low price. But the low price put smugglers and other merchants out of business. And the colonists were still required to pay the tax, which was three pence per pound of tea.

Of course, Edward was pleased to be chosen as an East India merchant. He foresaw great benefit for his business. Little did he consider the tender feelings of our neighbors. Some of his friends had to close their shops.

One night when he was away on business, the Sons of Liberty surrounded our house. They howled like Indians and shouted threats of violence. The cruelest cut was that my neighbors did nothing to aid me.

The following day, a mob gathered at Edward's shop. They put up a sign announcing Edward sold tea, as if this was a great crime. "Traitor!" they cried. Then they threw stones, shattering all the windows.

In the past few weeks, three ships filled with tea have sailed into Boston Harbor. The Sons of Liberty declared that the ships must go. They would not be allowed to unload their cargo. Boston would not pay the hated tax on tea.

Last night, on December 16, 1773, men dressed as Indians blackened their faces with soot. Carrying hatchets, they swarmed the ships. They tossed the tea into the sea. Though British soldiers were nearby, no one raised a hand to stop them.

Today is eerily quiet. I do not know what will become of us. Parliament's stroke is sure to be swift and terrible. My husband was **hung in effigy** outside his shop. He has told me we need to gather our things. It is no longer safe for him to have his shop here. We are off to Castle William, which is on an island in Boston Harbor. From thence where? To Canada? To England? I dread leaving all I have ever known.

▲ *Some colonists watched the Boston Tea Party from shore.*

I am a lover of peace. I fear this hatred of a three-pence tax on tea will have dreadful consequences. War will come to our shores again. This time the brave British soldiers will not protect us from our enemies. They will be our enemies. God save us all!

Thomas Brayson

British Soldier

My fingers are stiff from cold as I write this at Castle William. We of the 14th **Regiment** are stationed here at the fort. It is next to Boston Harbor, but we don't mix with the locals much. The Bostonians, an unruly people, are mighty unwelcoming of us. They cry foul over a three-pence tax on tea. I can feel no sympathy for them. At home in England, our rates are much higher.

Since the Seven Years' War ended, our economy has weakened. I am a weaver by trade, but my mill closed down. For weeks and weeks I looked for work with no success. My wife and four children grew hungry. Then the captain of my regiment came looking for new soldiers.

Thus I find myself here in Boston, a soldier of the foot in the British army. We soldiers must enlist for life. At least I joined of my own free will. Some here were **pressed** into service. They oftentimes need the lash to convince them to obey their officers.

Not that I blame them. A soldier's lot is a poor one. Our pay is barely enough to keep body and soul together. I try to find extra work, but this angers the Americans. They feel we take their jobs. There was a bit of a scuffle down at the docks the other day. Some of my comrades went round to look for work. The dockworkers took offense. They said the soldiers took bread from honest men's mouths. As if we British soldiers were not honest!

Americans claim that soldiers don't pay what they owe. Some say we even steal goods. One rumor has it that a soldier thumped a woman on the head and then stole her muff and bonnet while she lay senseless on the ground. An outrageous lie!

My friend Hugh was attacked by a mob because they said his commanding officer owed money for a wig. Truth was, the captain had paid his bill the day before. Poor Hugh was standing guard when ruffians began calling him names. They hurled snowballs, some filled with rocks. Others wielded clubs. Hugh called for help, and Captain Thomas Preston and seven soldiers rushed to his aid. In the turmoil, shots were fired. Five civilians were slain. The Sons of Liberty have called it a "massacre" to whip up the crowds. Rubbish! Our soldiers acted in self-defense.

▲ *British soldiers viewed the Boston Massacre as an unfortunate accident.*

BOSTON MASSACRE

British soldiers had been brought to the colonies in 1768 to enforce the Townshend Acts. Tension between the soldiers and colonists was high. On March 5, 1770, a fight broke out when a mob surrounded a group of soldiers. The soldiers fired on the crowd and five colonists were killed.

How these Sons of Liberty anger me! The vile organization is spread throughout the colonies, and I feel outraged when I see one of its members on the street. In my mind, men should be punished for this behavior, but their activities are not against the law, so we can do nothing. Here in Boston, Samuel Adams is their leader. They organize against Parliament, but I think it is a direct attack on our king.

It is said the group began in order to combat the Stamp Act. These colonists strongly disliked being forced to buy tax stamps for newspapers and playing cards. Well, we in England had to do it. Why not they? Still they managed to get the bill repealed with their boycotts. Now the power has gone to their heads. They will not accept any tax.

The Sons of Liberty tar and feather their opponents. This is a vile American torture, where they paint their victim with hot tar and cover him with feathers. Sometimes the Sons of Liberty stir the mobs to smash windows and destroy homes. All is done under the banner of lofty words. They cry for "freedom" and "no taxation without representation."

Now they have done their greatest mischief of all. Hundreds gathered in December 1773 to protest the landing of three ships loaded with tea. They would not pay Parliament's tax, which was due upon the unloading of these vessels. They claimed that bowing to the Tea Act would be like putting on the chains of slavery.

Instead they demanded that the loaded ships sail back to England. This the governor would not allow. So they dressed up like Indians and boarded the ships. They smashed the tea crates and threw the tea into the harbor. We awaited orders to protect the ships. The orders never came.

These so-called Indians destroyed 342 cases of tea, worth a good amount of money. Now they have a pretty price upon their heads. If no one comes forward to point out the guilty, the whole town will be held responsible. We will starve out the people of Boston until they pay back every penny. My country is not going to let this go unpunished.

We are being sent more soldiers to help us punish these cowardly rascals.

▲ *British soldiers were not present during the Boston Tea Party.*

Jonathan Pierce

Patriot Activist

I was but 14 when the Sons of Liberty rioted against the Stamp Act in 1765. I watched them gather outside the house of a **custom officer** and hang his stuffed image from a pole. They paraded it through the streets, stomped on it, and beheaded it. Then they returned to his home. They were pulling down his fence when my master discovered me. He took me by the ear back to the print shop where I served as apprentice.

The good of being a printer's apprentice was that I could read my fill. Through the words of important texts and my religious convictions, I came to believe that all men have the right to life, liberty, and property. A government's role is to provide for the good of all the people. Thus, the power of government must rest with the people, through a representative government. A Parliament an ocean away cannot know our ways here in the colonies. They cannot govern us.

I did not join the Sons of Liberty until after the British soldiers came to enforce the Townshend Acts in 1768. They were thrust upon us, **quartered** in our public buildings. This was a dreadful blow to our liberty.

The soldiers took a very high tone with us. More than one made an order at the shop, picked it up, and never paid the bill. When my master sent me to collect on one bill, the soldier and his comrades cuffed me.

The Sons of Liberty met to talk about ways to oppose Parliament's acts. ▶

They called me names and laughingly sent me on my way.

My friend and I saw a soldier alone outside the custom house. We got even by calling him names. "Bloody back!" we hollered. More of our friends came along and started hitting him with snowballs and other things. The soldier knocked down my friend with the butt of his rifle, and then a crowd gathered. Captain Preston and other soldiers came out of nowhere. We were giving it to them when shots rang out. The man beside me was shot in the back. I helped carry him to the doctor where he died.

That was in 1770. The soldiers eventually went to trial, but we got no satisfaction. Not a single member of the jury was from Boston. All but two of the soldiers were found not guilty. The guilty were **branded** on the thumbs and were released.

After that, I was eager to take up the cause. I often sit in the tavern and listen to the words of Samuel Adams. I even pen articles under a false name for our newspaper. I am no longer an apprentice. I am now a master myself and partner in the printing press. I am able to print the texts we Sons of Liberty need to spread our cause.

THINK ABOUT IT

▶ Determine the main idea of this paragraph and pick out one piece of evidence that supports it.

In the spring of this year, 1773, the British Parliament enacted the Tea Act. It gives the East

India Company full control of the tea trade, which would destroy our trade in the colonies. We would not abide by this limit to our freedom.

When three ships filled with tea docked in Boston, we knew we had to act. If the tea was landed, the duty would have to be paid. We would have bowed to the tyrant overseas. We stood guard round the ships to make sure no tea was unloaded.

On December 16, 1773, hundreds gathered at the Old South Meeting House. We sent a letter to the royal governor, asking that he allow the tea ships to sail back to England. Word came back that he refused. The cry went up, "Boston Harbor a tea-pot tonight!"

We spilled out of the hall and headed down to the wharf. Along the way, we stopped at the blacksmith's shop. There we blackened our faces with soot. We continued in silence and good order. British troops were stationed at Castle William by the harbor, but no one stopped us.

We divided in three. Each group boarded a ship. We requested from the captain the keys to the stores and some candles to light our way. He handed them to us, asking that we not damage the ship. We readily agreed.

Quietly we went about our work. We hoisted the tea chests out of the hold. Then we used our hatchets to smash each one open before tossing the damaged chests into the sea. Within three hours, all the tea was destroyed.

ANALYZE THIS

► Analyze two of the accounts in this book that detail when the tea was thrown into the water. How are they alike? How are they different?

As we left, I caught sight of a fellow stuffing tea into the lining of his coat. I grabbed his coat and shouted to the others. He tore away, leaving his coattail in my hand. But others caught him and threw his tea into the water.

Tea now lines the shore. In punishment, the British shut down Boston Harbor by passing the

Intolerable Acts. Parliament means to starve us until we pay for the tea we destroyed. Our sister colonies rally to our aid. They send food and goods overland to sustain us. Representatives from each of the colonies have gathered in Philadelphia to plan our course of action.

We have stockpiled weapons outside of Boston to protect ourselves. Governor Thomas Gage has sent soldiers to Lexington and Concord to try to capture the weapons.

I will join the militia. If I must, I will fight for my country. I will fight for freedom.

THE INTOLERABLE ACTS

As punishment for the Boston Tea Party, the British Parliament passed five laws, which Bostonians called the Intolerable Acts. Under the acts, Boston Harbor was closed until the town paid for the destroyed tea. Boston was placed under military rule, and British troops could now be quartered in the townspeople's homes without their consent.

LOOK, LOOK AGAIN

Take a close look at this illustration of the Boston Tea Party and answer the following questions:

1. What would a colonial merchant's wife who is loyal to England see in this picture? What would she think of the men tossing the tea overboard? Would she see them as heroes or villains? Why?

2. How would a British soldier describe this picture to his wife back in England? What would the soldier think when looking at this scene?

3. What would a patriot notice and think about this scene? How would the patriot think differently from the loyalist about the men who tossed the tea?

GLOSSARY

boycott (BOI-kaht) to refuse to buy goods or do business with someone as a form of protest

brand (BRAND) to burn a mark on the skin

custom officer (KUHS-tuhm AW-fi-sur) an official in charge of trade and collecting taxes at a port

East India Company (EEST IN-dee-uh KUHM-puh-nee) a British trading company

hang in effigy (HANG IN EH-fi-jee) to hang a dummy of someone, usually done in protest

legislature (LEG-is-lay-chur) a group of people who make or change laws for a city, state, or country

parliament (PAHR-luh-muhnt) a group of people who make or change laws in a country or state, such as the United Kingdom

press (PRES) to force someone into service

quarter (KWOR-tur) to house in a dwelling

regiment (REJ-uh-muhnt) a military unit made up of two or more battalions

Seven Years' War (SEV-un YEERS WOR) called the French and Indian War in the colonies, a war fought partly in America in which Austria, France, Sweden, and Russia fought Britain, Hanover, and Prussia for a number of territories

smuggle (SMUHG-uhl) to move goods into or out of a country illegally

LEARN MORE

Further Reading

Freedman, Russell. *The Boston Tea Party*. New York: Holiday House, 2012.

Gondosch, Linda. *How Did Tea and Taxes Spark a Revolution? And Other Questions about the Boston Tea Party*. Minneapolis, MN: Lerner, 2010.

Krull, Kathleen. *What Was the Boston Tea Party?* New York: Grosset & Dunlap, 2013.

Web Sites

Boston 1774
http://www.pbs.org/ktca/liberty/chronicle_boston1774.html
This Web site describes what happened after the Boston Tea Party.

Boston Tea Party
http://www.masshist.org/revolution/teaparty.php
This Web site explains more about the Boston Tea Party and shows documents from the time period.

INDEX

ABOUT THE AUTHOR

Linda Crotta Brennan has a master's degree in education. She has spent her life around books, teaching and working at the library. Now as a full-time writer, she loves learning new things and writing about them. Linda lives with her husband and their golden retriever. She has three grown daughters.

COMMON CORE ACTIVITIES

You need to learn about lots of things, but you also need to learn how to learn. This book encourages you to read and think critically about its content.

To guide your reading, this book includes notes that will help build the understanding and skills required by the Common Core State Standards. Look for the following callouts throughout the book:

- ▶ **Think about It:** The activities in this section ask you to interact with the book's content in ways required by the Common Core State Standards. You might be asked to identify a main idea, discuss surprising facts, or examine facts and ideas.

- ▶ **Analyze This:** These sidebars ask you to compare or contrast two or more of the narratives in the book to discover how they are similar or different.

- ▶ **Second Source:** These sections prompt you to find another source on this topic and compare the information there to the information in this source.